EVANGELISM:

THE CUTTING EDGE

GORDON CLINARD

HOME MISSION BOARD
Southern Baptist Convention
Atlanta, Georgia

Cover design: THOMAS H. BAKER

EVANGELISM:

THE CUTTING EDGE

CONTENTS

EVANGELISM:

THE CUTTING EDGE

the cutting edge

George Cornell of Associated Press and Douglas Johnson, a member of the American sociological association, carrying out a national survey, interviewed respondents representing fifteen major denominations. In all, they interviewed 3,454 persons, averaging one hour and fifteen minutes each. One of the questions discussed in each interview was, "What do you feel is the most important thing the church should be doing?" The answer that was first with all groups—blacks, whites, browns and minority groups—and was given the highest priority in the South, West, Northeast and the north central states was: "Winning others to Christ."

Larger churches did not rate evangelism quite as high as smaller churches. Rural and suburban churches rated evangelism higher than urban churches. But all groups placed evangelism first on the list of the church's priorities. For them, evangelism is the cutting edge.

Johnson and Cornell conclude: "Despite the peripheral differences, however, a consistent keynote, a common chord, stands out in regard to the main objective of the congregation. In total for all areas and groups, the cardinal concern is mediating on the message of Jesus, persuading others to believe and trust his unique authority and way." This seems to support what Hugo Culpepper has said: "The frontier of missions is that area between belief and disbelief." It may be found in every man. In short, evangelism is the work of the Holy Spirit in "convincing" men of sin, righteousness, and judgment.

This inclination of the lay person in the church to rate evangelism as the first priority of the church is seen as one of the marked trends in evangelism in the Southern Baptist Convention. The larger and traditionally influential churches, upon retirement of the religious statesman-type figure as pastor, are turning to young, more charismatic and more evangelistic-type persons. They are not nearly as concerned about Th.D.'s as they are about man's ability to build an evangelistic church.

This trend has not caught up with the denomination that seems to look for the religious statesman-type as the head of its institutions, but this probably will change drastically within the next decade. This ground swell of giving evangelism a new priority arises out of the lay people. It is a part of the dissatisfaction of lay persons with religious and irreligious technology. They are more concerned with a pastor's evangelistic gifts than with his denominational statesmanship.

In the sixties there was a growing dissatisfaction on the part of the laity with the evident lack of evangelistic success by the church. Pastors, not willing to admit that evangelism was dead, began to innovate in order to reach people. The bus ministry was a case in point. When materials and methods were not available within the denomination, churches did not hesitate to use and even adapt materials used by interdenominational or independent groups. By the advent of revival in the early months of the seventies, Southern Baptists already had models for evangelism. Innovative pastors with a unique personal magic in leadership soon were sought by more and more churches. The myth that the layman did not want to be involved was dispelled by evangelistic churches that demanded more and more of the layman's time in evangelistic visitation, bus ministry and witnessing projects.

The very group—the youth—who had been "turned off" to all religion became the agents of revival in the late sixties and first months of the seventies. What is more, they embraced a very radical brand of Christianity with great emphasis on evangelism, the Holy Spirit and the return of Jesus Christ. They no longer sought "rational" answers but demanded "feeling" in their faith. This was evidenced in their music, telling of a very personal love for Jesus. These young people brought with them from the age of protest a new concern for their fellows. "Jesus people," "street Christians" and "Spireno" became great factors in evangelism. The NOW generation had discovered Jesus Christ as the ONE way.

The awakening among young people, the desire for evangelistic success and the concern of the laity for a piece of the evangelistic action all were accompanied by a desire for personal purity and power. It was a cry for personal and church renewal. The big sins that stood in the way of this were no longer the old cardinal sins of sexual immorality, social drinking, card playing and theater going. There was a new concern with our personal relationships and our treatment of and attitude toward persons. It was now worse to be a slum landlord than a drunkard.

Out of this, in various forms, came the small group sessions. In these, personal honesty and personal relationships were exposed and brought under the searching gaze of God and others. Groups promoting personal and church renewal through renewal missions sprang up within and without the Southern Baptist Convention. This was a movement arising from the grass roots of the laity. It was both Spirit-filled and enthusiastic.

The four factors mentioned above were the milieu in which revival was born. Once again in the seventies, evangelism was an acceptable word. Many church and denominational leaders stopped searching for a graceful way to get out of evangelism. There was a new spirit and a new enthusiasm that began at the grass roots instead of in the denominational headquarters or in the pastor's study. It was great that the change had come, born of the Spirit.

This does not mean that all the dangers and hindrances to evangelism are removed. Indeed, in the very time when evangelism is "in," it is most beset by forces that can kill it. The problems are not with God or his gospel, but with men, churches and denominations. Men being what they are, there is always the danger that the work of God becomes prostituted by unworthy ambitions and by the desire for personal glory. Already there are signs that the desire to set new baptismal records and discover for ourselves personal reputations may be greater than our desire for the glory of God.

The Home Mission Board occupied a strategic role for Southern Baptists during the sixties. It took on a prophetic role by becoming a voice for social justice, racial equality and social ministry. And this prophetic stance did two important things in relation to missions and evangelism. First, it helped Baptist students in colleges and seminaries to see their denomination in a new light. *Home Missions* magazine became the most popular religious magazine in the school libraries. As a result, by the early seventies there were more young people knocking at the door of home missions than there was money to equip and send them—and this is still true.

Second, it pointed the way for the new evangelism with its theme that "people are big with God." The counter culture of the sixties had emphasized the importance of people. That persons are more important than computers or banks or corporations or success was carried over into the revival that sprang out of that counter culture. Today, largely because the Home Mission Board was courageous enough to accept its prophetic role, churches can discover methods and resources to "gird on the towel" in imitation of our Lord.

The program of evangelism development was assigned to the Home Mission Board. Between this program and those of interfaith witness, social ministries and church extension, housed in the same agency, there is a dynamic interplay of persons and programs. This working together helps to keep Southern Baptists on the one hand from going to the extremes of evangelism without social compassion and Christian understanding; and, on the other hand, it equally safeguards social work and interfaith dialogue from the absence of forthright Christian evangelism.

The overall purpose is "to bring men to God through Jesus Christ." Thousands of people are brought to Christ through the ministry of churches established through the work of the programs of church extension, Christian social ministries, language missions and others. Add to those the thousands won to Christ through specific evangelistic approaches, such as lay evangelism schools, revival crusades, youth and student evangelism and renewal evangelism weekends. The total adds up to the fact that the Home Mission Board is true to its basic objective.

Home missions *is* evangelism. This is the age of revival, and God is working miracles everywhere. His instruments are his churches and his people. Every Christian must become an evangelist and a trainer—one who motivates other evangelists. We may help an alcoholic. We may put an arm around a confused teen-ager. We may assist an unwed mother. We may minister to victims of drugs. We may move into an integrated neighborhood. We may protest injustice from the pulpit. We may love the unloving. But we will do it all in His name and be certain that He gets the glory.

JOHN HAVLIK

Chapter 1

a new boldness

No problem is more devastating in lay evangelism than the lack of proper motivation. Yet genuine motivation is not learned. It is a happening. It is the work of the Holy Spirit.

Laymen are motivated when they learn to celebrate what God in Christ has done for them daily. They are motivated when they are introduced to witnessing joy by someone who demonstrates rather than exhorts. The motivation seems to prevail among those laymen who sense they are a vital part in their church's mission—to win people to Christ.

Across the Southern Baptist Convention today increasing numbers of laymen—men, women, young people—are, with new enthusiasm, seeking and using their opportunities to share their faith with others. What is the secret of these changed lives? Where have they discovered this new boldness to witness? What has changed these people from intro verted timidity to outgoing love and concern? The answer is their discovery of a new motivation.

Awakened in the sixties from their long lethargy, laymen of every denomination began to reclaim as responsible members their preogatives in the life and work of their churches. They demanded to be heard and to have a slice of the action. Out of this movement came a rediscovery of the layman as a witness and the start of a new effort to equip him for his work. Among Southern Baptists, the Home Mission Board gave leadership to this movement.

There was adequate background for the effort. Elton Trueblood and Findley B. Edge had addressed themselves to this matter in many Baptist conferences and conventions. Pastors, like James Kennedy, minister of the Coral Gables Presbyterian Church of Fort Lauderdale, Florida, had set a pattern for training laymen to witness by a "one trains another" technique.

The Division of Evangelism of the Home Mission Board, carrying the program of evangelism development, had long been concerned about the inexhaustible resources in lay Christians for Christian penetration of society. After a study of churches and individuals, leaders in the division became convinced of two facts regarding the laity of the churches: First, the leaders were underestimating the desire of the lay person to become involved in direct forthright evangelism; and second, the pastor was underestimating the need of the average lay person for basic help in the area of personal witness.

Obviously, what the lay person needed was assistance in the form of training and new kinds of materials designed to be used on a person-to-person basis. What was sought was a transferable concept that could easily be used even by someone who was newly introduced to the faith. What was needed was a strategy for training the lay person.

Drawing on all the resources at hand, the division was

ready by the fall of 1970 to project its own venture in lay witnessing.

The thrust for this grew out of an earlier conference in Atlanta, attended by more than forty pastors, campus ministers, laymen, evangelism and other denominational leaders. Out of this meeting came the strategy for the lay evangelism school.

The training proposed demanded effective new materials. The original literature, called WIN (for *W*itness *I*nvolvement *N*ow) materials, was soon produced by the Church Training Department of the Sunday School Board in cooperation with the Evangelism Division. These included the witnessing tract, "How to Have a Full and Meaningful Life," follow-up letters which laymen could mail to those whom they led to Christ, four undated Sunday School lessons to be used in advance of the schools, leaflets designed to encourage Christians to grow through Bible study, and more advanced booklets dealing with various aspects of the Christian life.

The schools went through three phases of development. In phase 1 the training strategy and materials were tested in twelve pilot lay evangelism schools involving fifty churches throughout the Atlanta area. The congregations were inner-city, suburban and rural. A unique feature of the training were the lay leadership training schools, designed to train pastors and other leaders to conduct lay evangelism schools. For basic to the in-depth character of the training was the insistence that *no one* should lead a future school who had not first been trained as a participant in one himself.

The overwhelming response led the Evangelism Division to move into the second phase of their master plan. In phase 2 the schools were conducted in three other strategic cities: Houston, Chicago and Los Angeles. Hundreds of Christians were instructed in lay witnessing techniques in each city, with three thousand persons attending the sessions in Houston alone. As a result of this phase, reports show, the third largest number of baptisms in the history of the Southern Baptist Convention took place.

In phase 3 the states, under the leadership of state secretaries of evangelism, conducted thousands of schools throughout the nation, contributing to an even larger number of baptisms than had resulted from phase 2.

As the schools progressed, Jack Stanton, associate in the Division of Evangelism with special responsibility for the lay evangelism schools, said: "These meetings have proved the feasibility of our ultimate goal—to train laymen to train other laymen." By 1972 a definite goal had been set to instruct one thousand key laymen for the leadership of the evangelism training schools. Southern Baptists were geared up for a major thrust in personal evangelism.

Following the testing period, lay evangelism instruction was offered across the nation, in associations and churches. In 1972 the WIN materials had been translated into Spanish for use in the United States and in South and Central America. In September of the same year, Southern Baptists held their first lay evangelism schools in Europe, as a part of the Baptist World Alliance emphasis on the doctrine of world reconciliation. Since then, indicative of the vacuum of need which these materials have helped to fill, the WIN materials have been used effectively, with necessary adaptations, on many of our foreign mission fields to train lay Christians to witness to their own people.

The lay evangelism school is designed to assist a church to return to New Testament fundamentals. It seeks to answer the questions Who are we? and What does God want us to do? for both the individual and the church. We solve our identity crisis by rediscovering the simple New Testament answers to those questions: We are witnesses and We are to bear witness. Then the church is not fragmented by many abstract objectives, and it is free to be and do what

God wants it to be and do. This can be a great liberating experience for the church.

The lay evangelism school is a new and different approach for the church, because the emphasis is not on methods or materials but on *being* and *doing.* It uses only trained teachers who themselves have had the spiritual experience of a school. It offers content that strikes a balance between spiritual motivation and practical activities. Teaching methods include lectures, group dynamics and practical lab experiences. The experiences are evaluated for both the individual and the church.

Early it was learned that laymen who are beginning to share their faith in Christ need to visit with others who are already known and loved by a Christian congregation. Telephone surveys and more personal efforts to know such people proved to be rewarding. A Virginia pastor, discouraged with the prospects of church outreach, was overwhelmed to discover the large potential for witness and ministry in the church community. Another church began a crisis center, growing out of the discovery of great numbers of hurting people at the door of the church building.

Just as preparation for a school helped churches to be concerned about people, so some persons have found Christ because a church became interested in lay witness training. One twenty-four-year-old woman in San Diego had such an experience. Twice married and twice divorced, she had found little family support, for her mother was an alcoholic. She began to attend a small Southern Baptist church while they were conducting a lay evangelism school. She described her experience: "On the first day of the school, I became a Christian. I accepted Christ as my Saviour." She became interested in Bible study and began her Christian pilgrimage in a Christian fellowship that accepted her and gave her encouragement.

Lay evangelism schools follow a format which calls for maximum lay involvement. For four nights the sessions open with Bible study, stressing the Christian's life in Christ and its potential for spiritual maturity and service. The creative activity periods which follow these sessions have proved to be one of the most effective means of training. The best features of small group dynamics are used. Four people, usually not related as families and including a young person if possible, gradually learn how to express themselves openly and to become concerned about others. Such simple questions as: What do you associate with warmth in your home life? and When did God first mean something more than a word to you? have encouraged people to "open up" and to share with others.

In one school a woman could think only of a fireplace as the symbol of warmth in her childhood. Another thought of the love of her mother. Another person thought of the family meal, another of the fun time with his family, and another of the family prayer circle. As the group recalled the first time that God meant more than a word to them, they were forced to remember spiritual experiences which had long since been stored, like winter clothes in the summer, in their minds. The fresh memory often resulted in rededication.

The nightly sessions close with a witness-learning-action period. During this time the participants compose their verbal witness in brief statements and share them with other persons in training. In more than one case, this time has made laymen aware of their need to bring their Christian experiences up to date. In more than one school, leaders reported the conversion of people who faced up to the fact that they never had experienced new life in Christ.

On Thursday evenings members of the schools put their training into practice, as they visit in homes in the community and share their witness. One young woman who had never before spoken to another person about Christ selected a neighbor as the one she would visit. But as Thursday night approached, she became more and more nervous about the visit. On Thursday morning she could wait no longer. Hopping on her bicycle, with her baby riding in the front basket, she rushed to her neighbor's house. When her friend learned of her purpose, she said, "I am so glad that you came. I've been hoping a long time someone would tell me about how to become a Christian." One nervous Christian found a thrilling beginning to what hopefully will become a lifetime of effective witness.

Laymen have found all kinds of opportunities and problems to challenge them during the visitation assignments. These experiences are shared when the group return from their calls. Many tell of resistance which has crumbled when people have learned that the visitors did not come merely to talk about attending church. Two men reported that they were about to leave a house when the man they had come to see drove up. When they told him they had come to talk about Christ, he bristled in resistance. They did not panic but spoke naturally of their relation to Christ and of their concern for the man. He invited them into his home, and soon he told them that he was a professing Christian, but that he had not been baptized or joined a church. Before they left, their new friend had made a fresh Christian commitment and had spoken favorably about uniting with the church of his choice on the following Sunday.

Christians learn in the Thursday visitation not to be discouraged by closed doors. In one sharing session a woman asked if those who had refused to listen to her witness should be forgotten. Others in the group reminded her of Jesus' story of the shepherd who searched diligently for one lost sheep. She determined to find some way, perhaps through others who knew the persons to whom she had spoken, to continue her ministry of concern.

New evidences of an "unhindered" gospel breaking across all barriers have come from the testimonies of Christians who are involved in witness for the first time. One man related the breakdown of one of his prejudices. He had just witnessed to his first black. With emotion he said, "When that man accepted Christ as his Lord, black was beautiful!" Others learn the value of a casual moment with a stranger. In a brief moment, after a Christian man had given a high school student a ride, they were in front of the young man's school. The man gave the student the witnessing leaflet and started to let him out of the car, but the words the man had learned in the lay evangelism school he attended haunted him: "If you don't have eight minutes in which to share with someone your experience with Christ, perhaps you are living too fast." He asked the boy to get back in the car so that he could share the witnessing leaflet with him. The boy made a profession of faith in Christ. The layman learned the lesson that the Christian needs to be sensitive to the leadership of the Holy Spirit in taking advantage of a casual contact with someone who needs Christ.

The Evangelism Division has set the highest goal of all when lifetime dedication to Christian witnessing has been the object of every school's ministry of training.

As the lay evangelism schools have continued, methods have been refined and new materials have been added. By 1973 churches were spending eighteen weeks of careful preparation in advance of the five-day, ten-hour evangelism training week. Churches were also devoting more time to follow-through training of laymen and of new Christians. This latter effort was aimed at the greatest single necessity in evangelism: the conservation of those who are won to Christ for active participation in the Christian life.

Because many churches as well as individuals involved in lay evangelism experienced a renewal element, leaders of the Evangelism Division saw the need to tie these two—renewal and evangelism—more closely together. Out of this, renewal evangelism was born. This is a process or journey into wholeness through which churches help their people to become more alive as witnesses and ministers of Jesus Christ. Renewal keeps evangelism deep and whole, while evangelism keeps renewal from being introverted and subjective.

Along with the lay evangelism schools, the Evangelism Division began a ministry of lay renewal. This action acknowledged that revival always precedes evangelism. It seeks to waken laymen spiritually, so they will become motivated for their ministry of witness. It also aims at the revival of evangelism as a laymen's movement, just as lay evangelism schools have done.

Reid Hardin, associate director in the Home Mission Board's Division of Evangelism, is the staff member charged with providing renewal evangelism resources to churches, associations and state conventions. He is himself a layman—the only layman ever to be appointed to the evangelism staff. Former director of Layman's Landing, a renewal fellowship center near Deerfield Beach, Hardin came out of the business world. He gained experience by participating in lay renewal conferences and retreats and lay evangelism schools in Texas, Alabama and Florida.

Hardin and others enthusiastic over the lay renewal idea travel across the United States, leading renewal weekends in churches of different sizes, in different types of locations and situations. A small, rural church in Texas experienced renewal during a weekend of fellowship together. A visiting lay team of men and women from the Southeast led the church members, young and old, in small group sessions, testifying times and creative worship. Luncheons, ice cream socials and games of miniature golf brought the people together in a relaxed celebration-atmosphere. Their theme, "God loves you and I love you," was more of an experience than a statement.

During one service a long-haired youth stood and said, "Age has not been a barrier in this meeting; in the past it has been something that has really hung up this church. I'm so glad we have all come together." Released from restraining tensions, teen-agers hugged parents, expressing love and asking forgiveness for past hurts. Deacons rushed forward to show appreciation to their pastor. Old friends embraced and expressed long-suppressed gratitude for each other.

Hardin believes that if real Christlike love were released across the nation, evangelism would result from the overflow. "Everyone everywhere," he says, "would point to Christians and say 'Look, how they love one another.' "

The goal of church-centered lay renewal weekends, lay witness missions and other lay-related events is "life-style evangelism," defined by Hardin as "Christians using every relationship of life to share the good news of Jesus Christ with other persons in those relationships. It is Jesus Christ himself reaching out, spiritually awakening persons as they are 'fleshing out' the good news."

Life-style evangelism, Hardin explains, "is developed in the loving community of the local church, as new and renewed Christians mature in an atmosphere of openness, acceptance and affirmation." From the church, Christians venture out into the world, carrying with them their life style of evangelism, "equipped to verbalize their faith within a hurting and broken world."

In the fall of 1972 forty-nine renewal evangelism associates were appointed. During 1973 that number was increased to one hundred. These were all laymen—men and women—committed to give priority for two years to training in lay renewal techniques and participation in lay renewal weekends. At the same time, they were each committed to training ten additional persons in lay renewal. Eventually these persons formed teams of regional resource persons ready to train and recommend to the churches fifty thousand resource people throughout the Southern Baptist Convention.

David Haney, a renewal associate and author of a group study book entitled *Renew My Church,* describes renewal as "the liberation of the laity." The idea is that the pastor equips the congregation for ministry, rather than the congregation existing to support the pastor. "It's the difference between a torchbearer and a lamplighter," Haney says. "The idea we operate under now is that we are all torchbearers and the pastor is the guy out front. But the lighter of lamps is the guy who lights many lamps and sends them out."

Renewal evangelism and lay evangelism schools go hand-in-hand. A large Baptist church in Virginia became aware of a need for spiritual renewal as the date for a lay evangelism school approached. The church's leadership feared for the support of the school, for, until this time, laymen had not been actively involved in outreach. The Virginia city was not generally open to the door-to-door type of visitation which lay evangelism schools encourage. But the hunger for spiritual renewal had begun months before concern for the success of the training week had surfaced.

The church had a history of outstanding mission support. Its staff had always been excellent. But the congregation was steeped in tradition. For some time, in small groups, laymen had expressed a desire for a more fulfilling Christian life. They wanted something into which they could thrust themselves in ministry and Christian growth.

When these concerns surfaced, the church decided to plan several renewal meetings before the lay evangelism school was scheduled to open. A team of laymen from Florida, Arkansas and the Carolinas visited the church. Members of the team served as catalysts in small and large group meetings involving a cross section of the church. Renewal came, and it involved many in the church. As a result, more than two hundred church members were in the lay evangelism school. The chairman of the deacons said that because of the experience he felt a depth in his Christian life he had never known before.

Reid Hardin points out two things that happened in the church: One, there was a growth in the sense of need to create an awakened fellowship in which people could relate to one another and thus provide a basis for outreach to the community; and, two, people who had not before been inclined to witness to the lost or to make them welcome in the church became part of the ministry of outreach.

In Texas a church had a similar experience. For years the congregation had participated in laymen's revivals and soul-winning study courses. Results had been limited. Thoughtful members expressed a need for something more. Prayerfully, the pastor and staff enlisted more than two hundred people who were interested in a renewal mission. They met for prayer each Sunday for several weeks.

One February night, ninety laymen arrived in the city for the weekend. They were coordinated by a truck driver from Alabama. Seven hundred church members met them for dinner that Friday evening. The fellowship meal was followed with a worship service. Then team members began to give their testimonies. This was followed by small sharing groups which met for an additional half hour.

Coffees were held on Saturday morning. At numerous luncheons many persons joined team members in sharing examples of God's recent blessings and guidance. Other worship and small group sharing followed on Saturday evening. Sunday morning the team coordinator gave his testimony in the worship hour.

That evening, with team members gone, the church met to evaluate, to share what God was doing, and to give thanksgiving for answered prayer. High school and junior high school students joined with adults in expressing their joy in renewal. In the weeks that followed, testimony became a part of the church's life. It was not uncommon for a person to ask for prayer and to find members of the church gathered about him, placing their hands on his shoulders and praying with him. One man said, "I have been a Christian for forty years and this has been the greatest spiritual experience of my life." The entire spiritual life of the church changed. A new sense of God's presence prevailed in every worship service. Attendance and giving increased. Many people were won to Christ and were baptized. Revivals had new power. Renewal among young adults was especially remarkable.

These examples demonstrate the strategy and the result of renewal evangelism now projected by the Evangelism Division. This needed ministry is built on two essential principles: First, evangelistic witness begins with awakening experiences. Second, awakened persons begin to share in a fellowship which creates not only an authentic evangelistic atmosphere but also the environment of spiritual maturity.

Hardin and other staff members of the Evangelism Division see their role as resource persons. "We are coordinators on a national level to help people find the resources that God is raising up through the grass roots. Here, resources of renewal are being born." From a national perspective Hardin sees the need to relate some of these resources to traditional Baptist life. "Our role is to touch these, seek them out, find out where renewal is happening, and correlate those things that relate responsively to Baptist needs, making these available to churches."

These new emphases in evangelism helped Southern Baptists in 1972 to break all previous records for baptisms.

Chapter 2

a revolutionary move

A popular athlete and excellent student approached the campus minister at a university in the Midwest. He and a fraternity brother had begun a Bible study. More than twelve other men were now involved, and they needed materials to help them. When the minister visited with the group, he found the boys relaxed in their familiar fraternity house environment, sharing their understanding of the Bible and of their growing Christian maturity in a remarkable way.

There is nothing unusual about this scene today. In the last few years a revolutionary move toward the Christian faith, with emphasis focused on the person of Jesus Christ, has characterized the student world on the college campus. The new interest has come in the midst of the continued strong drug culture, popularity of Eastern religions, and occupation with the occult such as astrology, witchcraft, and Satan worship. Young people now freely share their faith with each other in small group and commune settings. This upsurge of interest going on in the college culture has great significance for Christian evangelism and the ministry of the church. What has caused the change?

In the sixties college campuses were often places of extreme concerns, violently expressed. They rocked under student force, resulting in sometimes destructive demonstrations against such issues as student anonymity, racism, poverty, war in Vietnam and hunger. The pattern was crusade for change! The descriptive word was involvement NOW! Because involvement often meant violence, blood frequently flowed across proud and stately university campuses.

All symbols of authority and establishment, including the church as well as the government, were discarded. No authority figure was unchallenged. The Bible and the existence of God were questioned and tossed aside. The church was rejected as a hypocritical defender of the status quo when it should have been, the critics insisted, the crusader for social and political reformation. They accused the church of hypocrisy in such basic Christian concepts as honesty, love and compassion. Their discarding of value systems was flaunted before the world.

When disillusionment with violent protest as the means of righting the wrongs of the world came at last, the under-thirty generation found themselves staring into a way of life that offered no hope or foundation on which to stand. Instead of solving problems, it compounded them. Inevitably there was a change—surprising and radical in its direction and impact. Young people by the hundreds turned from a grossly secular style of life to one that was distinctly spiritual as the Jesus Movement began to sweep the land. Even with its excesses, the presence of the Spirit of God was evident in the movement. Undeniable, genuine conversions gave evidence to the spiritual forces at work.

The Jesus people went everywhere, including the modern college campus. Young people by the thousands were caught up in the movement. They found an ability to speak of their faith. They demonstrated an unusual love for one another. They were concerned with the importance of people as persons as they witnessed.

Stung and shaken by the violent accusations and rejection of the young people, churches in every denomination began to look deep within themselves—and found themselves wanting. They began to listen to, and to hear, what the young people were saying. With new honesty many set about to make their own change. When the NOW generation began to return to the established churches they had rejected, they found in hundreds of them a new warmth and affirmation, a new openness and freedom in expressing loving concern and acceptance of one another. They found a new willingness to express and share one's faith in Jesus Christ.

During these years evangelism had fallen on difficult days on the college campus, as it had elsewhere. It was interesting, however, to note that even during this time young people had continued to respond to such organizations as the Peace Corps and Vista. Southern Baptists found excellent response to innovative mission services such as the US-2 ministry and student summer missions, revealing that this generation remained ready to respond to a challenge that required investment of self in a Cause.

By the seventies, students had again begun to work within the "establishment" to attempt to achieve the goals they considered worthy. They gained the right to vote at the age of eighteen and took active part in politics. One of the strongest efforts in the national election of 1972 was the fight by the political parties for the youth vote.

Student reaction toward religion in general and the Christian faith in particular changed dramatically. Nathan Porter, associate in the Evangelism Division, in charge of

Student Evangelism, states that three things characterize the contemporary college generation's attitude toward Christianity.

College students are open to the gospel. It has become easy to talk about Jesus Christ. Popular songs in 1972 were full of his name. *Jesus Christ Superstar,* however open it was to theological criticism, played to packed houses from New York to California. This new openness to the gospel opened the door for a campus evangelism which has integrity and appeals to the whole person.

When a nervous pair of Christian coeds at a university knocked on the door of a dormitory room, they found three girls "putting on their faces" to go out to a favorite bar. One was Jewish, another Catholic, and the other had no religious background at all. When the Christian girls politely offered to return at a more convenient time, they were requested to stay. After more than an hour of conversation about the Christian faith, the Jewish girl insisted that her new friends come again. The nervous witnesses for Christ learned that their classmates were surprisingly open and ready to talk about the meaning of faith.

Students have a vital new interest in understanding the Bible and their beliefs. Some campus ministers have distributed more than a thousand Bibles and study materials dealing with the Christian life. Bible study groups have broken out all over campuses—especially in the college community where it has been difficult to penetrate with an evangelical witness before. Bible study has brought many to full commitment to Christ, as well as strengthening the faith of students already Christian. A young woman at an east Texas university bought a Bible. Two weeks later she came to the Baptist student director to say, "I have studied this book alone. Something is happening in my life. I have given up drugs, and I have written my boyfriend to tell him that, like it or not, he will find me a different girl."

Porter identifies the third characteristic of the college

scene in the early seventies as a new interest of Christians in learning to share their faith effectively. Large numbers are eager to witness on campus. And their motivation is one of genuine concern. In Texas more than twenty thousand Southern Baptist young people attended conferences on personal witnessing sponsored by the Texas Baptist Convention. They prayed together, studied together, and shared their faith on the streets.

One great cause for the new interest among young people in the Christian faith is their feeling of loneliness. They are open to confess that a vacuum exists in their lives, in spite of the technology and in spite of the drug and sex culture which has dominated modern society. Man is more than physical. He is a spiritual being, and the youth of the nation admit that something is missing in life if the spiritual dimension is ignored. This very fact has opened the door for campus invasion by the demonic. But it has also opened the door for authentic Christian evangelism.

Some time ago, in a Baptist college chapel service, an associate in a state Baptist division of student work invited all present to turn to another and say, "God loves you and has a place for you in Jesus Christ." A young woman spoke to a student who was seated not far away. The sentence opened the door for a conversation with the young man. He was lonely in the midst of a crowd, as so many people are. The spiritual side of his life had been neglected, and he was a stranger to any real joy. The conversation led to other visits. Other students demonstrated that they cared for him. Within a short time, he had committed his life to Christ.

Under the mask of self-sufficiency and new-found freedom, most students are really lonely. This emptiness, which screams loudest after the stimulation of drugs, alcohol, or any other superficial "upper" wears itself out, has created an openness to Christ.

Baptist student ministries have given a good account of themselves for years. They have led many to Christ, they have deepened the commitment of many Christians, and they have related student ministry to the churches. Now they have taken advantage of new student openness to lead in campus evangelism. The Evangelism Division of the Home Mission Board serves these existing organizations through their departments of campus ministries and in cooperation with the National Student Ministries of the Sunday School Board of the Southern Baptist Convention.

The principles and techniques of the lay evangelism movement have become the basic thrust on campus also. Because young people were the agents of revival, every effort has been made to involve them with adults in the local congregations in personal witnessing. One spin-off from lay evangelism was the demand for training of campus minsters in the techniques of lay evangelism schools. In answer, the Division of Evangelism led in the training of every Southern Baptist campus minister in one large state, while other states sent their campus ministers to lay evangelism schools.

To meet the need, Nathan Porter designed materials—adapted from those used in the schools—which included a transferable concept witnessing booklet, "Life with Meaning and Purpose," and a strategy for lay witnessing on the campus. Twenty Bible study folders with an evangelistic thrust were in use by thousands of students in the years 1971 through 1973.

The goals of spiritual growth, witness training and follow-up remain the same. Students are encouraged to become involved in church lay evangelism schools and to conduct similar efforts on the campus.

Spiritual growth is sought through Bible study. Small groups meet for six weeks, and some for as long as a year, to do in-depth study of the Scriptures. Both Christians and non-Christians have responded in all segments of the campus culture. The goal is to involve the entire student body, in groups or individually, in Bible study.

The evangelism training seminar, similar to the lay evangelism school, is an intensive week designed to help students to share their faith. The sessions are usually scheduled for three days and include from eight to ten hours of training. The first six to eight hours are given to equipping the students to witness; the remaining hours are devoted to actual witness experience. This training includes hints on making friendship valuable for witnessing and instruction in beginning a conversation and turning it in the direction of sharing a Christian testimony. The witnessing booklet is the primary tool. There are also multiple booklets for new as well as for maturing Christians. They cover such subjects as love, sin, the Holy Spirit, devotional life, the Christian life, the Christian witness, the church, Jesus Christ, the new birth, and man. The student response to these seminars has been exciting.

At the University of Illinois, when the evangelism training seminar began, ten Bible study groups had been meeting for weeks. More than twenty-five students enlisted for training in witness. At Baylor University the training seminar was scheduled for the third week of the busy fall term. Four hundred students were trained to share their faith more effectively.

College students have sometimes come to grips with their own needs to become Christians in the small sharing groups which are a part of the evangelism training seminar. An attractive young woman, attempting to share her faith in a group meeting, recognized that she had no witness to give. Reared in church, she was now a student in a Christian college. She thought herself to be a Christian. But now there was nothing real that she could say about her daily life with Christ. Before the sharing group was concluded, she found Christ in a vital, personal way for the first time. She is one of many who, in an effort to express their faith, have found faith for themselves.

The third phase of campus education for witness is the long-term "E Group" ("E" for evangelism) training. The students and a leader meet for more than an hour each week for ten weeks to continue Christian growth experiences. Skills in sharing Christ are deepened by the discussion of problems and personal experiences in talking with people about Christ. During the ten weeks, members of the groups are encouraged to witness to five college students, three high school students and two persons in the community. They also begin Bible study groups on the campus.

The adaptations of the lay evangelism school were made with the problems and hang-ups of college students in mind. The best emphasis is on building friendships as the basis for Christian witness. A psychiatrist, who has worked closely with students involved in earlier disorders at Harvard and who has seen many of their lives change completely from a secular life style to full commitment to Christ, has said, "The most effective witness to them will be the knowledge of what Christ has done and is doing in the lives of other young people."

Nathan Porter makes another point: "Campus evangelism has to be flexible. It can never be taken for granted that students will not change. Christian students must be sensitive to changing situations. They must remain open and, above all, they must not reject people." But the strategy of campus evangelism continues to involve students in personal evangelism on many college and university campuses.

High school evangelism also had to be included in any consideration of youth's response to the Christian faith, for these young people had demonstrated that they too were excited about Bible study and evangelism. Many had participated in lay evangelism schools. In 1971 Barry St. Clair was added to the staff of the Division of Evangelism and began to research the needs of high school youth—recognized as the most important single group of instruments for revival and renewal.

During the year, two training events, Super Summer '72 held in the summer and Christmas Challenge held during

Christmas week, reached hundreds of high school youth, changing their lives and leading them to make commitments to deeper Christian living and to evangelize their high schools.

Super Summer '72 was held on Furman University campus for two three-week terms. These were planned to help teen-agers to identify and to understand their own personal experiences with Jesus, to learn how to witness, and to study a strategy for penetrating their own schools with the gospel. These weeks combined inspiration, training and recreation. Through Bible study sessions, small-group training in discipling, and participation in actual experiences witnessing in the community, the lives of several hundred youth were transformed. Participation in a parks ministry in cooperation with the city parks department, resulted in almost fifty professions of faith being made.

The real tests came as these teen-agers returned to their homes. Typical of many was one young man who had come to Super Summer "just to get away from home." He returned, on fire with purpose for the first time in his life, to lead his own church into a new evangelism emphasis and outreach. Others, with changed lives testified to by parents, led their peers to know Jesus Christ. One girl from Virginia returned home to learn that her father had terminal cancer. She was able to lead him to faith in Christ before he died. She wrote that she felt God had sent her to Super Summer to prepare her for her father's death and to learn that she could rejoice at his salvation.

During Christmas vacation that same year, seven hundred high school students and youth workers gathered in Atlanta for Christmas Challenge, a shortened version of Super Summer. Witness training sessions and Christian growth experiences were at the heart of the program. A project, in cooperation with Economic Opportunity, took the teen-agers into an Atlanta ghetto where they painted seventeen rooms and witnessed to the tenants. One new

Christian who participated in a two-day street clean-up campaign, sponsored by the Christmas Challenge group, shared his faith so effectively that seven people accepted Christ.

While Christmas Challenge was a one-time project, Super Summer was repeated in 1973, this time on six college campuses in different regional areas.

St. Clair's philosophy for youth evangelism is "to share Jesus Christ with high school students through the local church." To do this, he has developed on the youth level the equivalent of lay evangelism schools on the adult. One of his problems has been to work out terminology and a vocabulary that would communicate with the age level. Evangelism training is embodied in what is called, for youth, the reach out ministry.

A twelve-week project, reach out teams that are similar to "E" groups in Student Evangelism provide in depth what Super Summer compresses into three weeks. Under the leadership of youth leaders in a church, it is designed to be used by any church, or any group within a church, to train high school students to carry out a youth evangelism ministry in high schools. Piloted in two churches, one in Georgia and one in North Carolina, the ministry has proved highly successful.

One of the leaders in the Georgia project said: "Kids are tired of playing games. The days are gone when you can pass out the ping pong ball and open the soft drink machine and call that a ministry. Reach out is geared to truth—living Christianity in a consistent and effective way."

This is one of St. Clair's personal goals in the youth evangelism program of the Home Mission Board. "I want high school students," he says, "to know that God can transform their entire lives, if they will let him."

Evangelism training is carried on through other types of activities. Under encouragement from the Home Mission Board, several hundred church youth choirs have for years converted their tours into witness missions, using music and personal witnessing as their means of communicating the gospel message. Porter and others in the Evangelism Division have on occasion given assistance and counsel in advance training and preparation of the teen-agers for these tours. At one time fifty-three young people from South Main Baptist Church in Houston worked, in cooperation with the Missions Division of the Board, in a language mission crusade in the greater Hartford, Connecticut, area. Like many other youth choirs, this one financed its own trip by saving trading stamps, collecting and selling old newspapers, having garage sales, washing cars, cleaning windows, baby-sitting and doing odd jobs. These Christians are a vital part of the emerging student response to spiritual maturity and witness.

Beach and resort area ministries tell another of the thrilling stories of contemporary campus evangelism. Beach projects at Fort Lauderdale and Daytona Beach, Florida, during the now famous college spring vacation weeks are typical. These projects are sponsored by Student Evangelism of the Home Mission Board, in cooperation with the National Student Ministries, the Florida Baptist Convention and the local Baptist associations.

Thousands of students flee the college campuses each year, many of them from the still unthawed north, for days on the beach in the sun and nights in the motels, where color television, drinking and sex are the major pastimes. One year, five hundred Baptist students from more than twenty states and forty-five campuses came to the beaches to witness. Under Porter's leadership, workshops in evangelism were conducted in the mornings. In the afternoons, the students mingled with the crowds on the beaches, swimming, making new friendships and giving testimonies for Christ. Coffeehouses, open in the evenings, were the big attraction. Students came to enjoy free sandwiches and orange juice, to hear music and to talk about many things, including their ideas about God.

Two hundred made professions of faith on the Florida beaches during that spring college break. Christian students shared their witness with over five thousand others. It is of great interest to learn that the students who reported professions of faith were largely those who had shared their witness with only five to eight other persons. This speaks strongly about the importance of building friendships, of listening to others, and of patience in effective Christian evangelism.

Some of the more creative hours of witness were those spent in the coffeehouses on the beaches. In one, the tables were covered with white paper. Crayons were available at each table. People drew, wrote poetry, or "doodled" in general. This "art" produced excellent chances for evangelistic witness. One student from Florida State sat at a table with four young men. He drew a tree and labeled it "tree of life." His four friends began to put things on the tree which they felt were important for life. They drew leaves for such things as money, sex, family, an education and work.

As they talked, one student remarked, "It seems like God should be on the tree somewhere." "Where should we put him?" the Christian asked. "I suppose he should be above all of life," the first student responded. They drew God above the tree.

When someone asked, "How do you get God in your life?" the Christian had the chance to tell the group how God comes into a human life. Before they left the coffeehouse, one of the young men had joined the Florida State student in the discovery of new life.

A Canadian, obviously a thoughtful student, summed up the worth of witnessing built upon established friendships: "I am thrilled to see how the Holy Spirit can use kids who are committed. But there is a danger in treating people like objects. We can't befriend a person simply for the purpose of bringing him to Christ. This is not what Christ would do. Christ drew all to him by his example, love and attitude. He befriended out of interest in a *person*. This love can only be given by the Holy Spirit. Then let the Holy Spirit work to open the door to communicate the gospel."

One who found Christ in the beach ministry confirmed the Canadian student's observation. "The people who helped me," he said, "were those who did not talk to me directly about the Lord, but who showed me what he meant. Those were the people who influenced me in coming to Christ."

The experience of witnessing in a beach ministry has a way of deepening the Christian's own spiritual life. One student confessed, "I looked on the beach ministry as a chance to get away. But my own life has been 'cleared out.' I am the one who has grown." Another agreed. "I have learned to be myself, to be real, to be sensitive to others." One excited student found that "Jesus is alive in Fort Lauderdale. All we need to do is to let him out of jail and do his work!" Many who came to the beaches were determined to return home to continue their witness through their churches.

The inspiration of the Florida beach ministries has led to similar work in other areas. Texas Baptist students have conducted witness missions at Galveston and other beach resorts for some years. In Kentucky a group of more than two hundred students, working through the Campers on Mission ministry of the Board, determined to conduct Bible studies and to share their faith at such resort areas as the Land Between the Lakes, Mammoth Cave, and Cumberland Falls. Local church groups of college and high school students have begun similar ministries near their homes.

Across the nation the picture on campus seems clear. Students reaffirm that all Christians can share their faith.

Chapter 3

a whole gospel

Executive Secretary Arthur B. Rutledge of the Home Mission Board, in a meeting with editors of state Baptist papers, delineated the relationship between evangelism and Christian social ministries. He outlined the Board's national mission strategy, emphasizing the Board's commitment to cross all barriers to make disciples of Christ. Among the barriers named were social and moral problems. The executive secretary stated that top priorities in a national mission strategy are church extension, evangelism and social ministries.

The statement suggests that the lack of social ministries is a hindrance to making disciples. It also sees evangelism and social ministries as belonging to the same mission strategy. Both views are biblical. Evangelism and social ministry belong together.

The gospel is addressed to man as a total person. This is

significant for man's relation to other men as well as for his relation to God. And God is concerned about social as well as personal redemption. In *The Greening of the Church,* Southern Baptist leader of Christian renewal Findley Edge has said, "The emphasis on the physical-social needs of man is not simply a 'desirable addition' to a gospel that at its base is 'spiritual.' The point is that this social emphasis is just as integral and necessary a part of the gospel as the evangelical emphasis."

Edge went on to say that "those who insist that the basic task of the church is to 'save souls' are just as wrong in their view as are those who believe that the primary task is to meet the human needs of man. Either emphasis alone—or out of proportion—is inadequate."

Jesus never neglected man's basic need for reconciliation with God. But he crossed all barriers of race, culture, economics and poor religion to bring healing to man's pain. He stood against everything which threatened the freedom and integrity of men.

Jesus' intent was clearly enunciated in a statement presented by a Southern Baptist to the Continental Congress on Evangelism in 1968. After affirming Christ as the world's only hope and the validity of personal conversion and salvation, the paper also affirmed that "the gospel must be related to the needs of daily life and interpersonal relations. Within the fold of the church the disinherited of the earth are to be regarded as children of God and as of infinite worth. The gospel cannot tolerate injustice or man's inhumanity to man."

Known for their enthusiastic evangelism, Southern Baptists have long been involved in the social aspect of Christian discipleship. Historically, they have expressed their social interest through hospitals; colleges; homes for the aged, unwed mothers and children; Baptist centers; rescue missions; and morally significant political struggles. In later years these have been expanded into more contemporary areas of man's needs.

Through these and other services, Southern Baptists have extended Christian compassion to those harmed by social injustice and physical need. This is social concern. In addition, in many instances the forces of local churches and the denomination have moved to eliminate the evil causes which bring about human suffering and injustice. This is social action. Through such concern and action many persons have found their greatest opportunity to lead others to Christ. The indications are that the current renewal of evangelism is accompanied by renewal of emphasis on social ministry opportunities which confront Christians.

Home Mission Board's John Havlik, associate in the Evangelism Division, suggests that evangelism is the cutting edge of the Christian mission. The definition implies that the church has one mission—to *be* the people of God in the world, to *do* the will of God on earth. Under this "umbrella" all aspects of the Christian task can be placed. Evangelism is the cutting edge of the mission, because to evangelize is to make disciples. But social ministry is another part of the same mission.

Genuinely evangelistic churches generally are those which are actively engaged in some forms of social ministry. For years one congregation had done well to "hold their own" in a rapidly changing community. It was also surviving in the struggle to retire a large building indebtedness. Recently, the church took a new look at priorities and goals for the future and decided that their primary mission was outreach.

Every energy was turned in the direction of making Christian disciples. In the process, renewed interest in evangelism multiplied the church's social ministries. As the Christians ministered to the spiritual needs of the ethnics and sometimes to low-income groups in the community, they found themselves involved in caring for these people as total persons. As a result, the church brought more persons to a knowledge of Christ than they had done in years. They became heavily involved in ministering to the human hurts about them and, as they did, in political and social action to eliminate the causes of the hurts.

Too often witnessing has been deterred by the attitudes and actions of Christians themselves. It has fallen on deaf ears because genuine concern for men as individuals was lacking. Churches, like individuals, in our contemporary culture must win the right to be heard. And Christians must care before men will listen to their personal testimony to the love and power of Christ in human life.

Admittedly we may salve our consciences for our lack of evangelism mission by relying upon the witness of "life" rather than by verbal expression. For as Findley Edge has stated, "It is possible to engage in social action as a means of evading the necessity of confronting an individual with his need for personal salvation." Either extreme is in error. But likely the greater Christian danger at the moment is a failure to demonstrate concern by action in the interest of man's total needs.

A North Carolina pastor's experience illustrates the way the lack of social concern and action can become a barrier to evangelism. For years his congregation had been content to baptize their own growing children, to build the necessary buildings, and to give as much to missions as possible. All of these were worthy, indeed. But they reached few adults for Christ and practically no one outside the church family. Concerned about their loss of credibility in telling the good news of the gospel, the church put usual evangelism methods aside for a time. The membership searched their souls about their concern, first for one another, then for others. Following a period of repentance and renewal, they began to be involved in social ministries in the community. They worked as a church and in cooperation with other churches and with existing community social service agencies. They offered their church building as the meeting place for youth seeking help in the growing battle with drugs.

Months later evangelism had taken on new life, for the

church members had found new and natural ways to witness as they ministered to people's hurts. On the other hand, as people outside saw a church concerned about them as persons, many sought the secret of the spirit of love that was exhibited. In this, they found commitment to Christ.

Underlying all that the Home Mission Board does is the conviction that bringing men to Jesus Christ is basic. This purpose is at the heart of every program of work. Each is designed to help cross barriers so that men may become Christ's disciples. Every department of work, along with the Division of Evangelism, is a part of the one Christian mission, to be the people of God in the world that others might come to him.

In no department is this more evident than in Christian Social Ministries. In the four years between 1969 and the end of 1972 this department reported over fourteen thousand conversions with more than 6,598 additions to the churches. Such services as weekday ministries, family life concerns, literacy ministries, work with drug addicts and alcoholics, concern for prisoners and those just released from prison, and other social ministries provide unlimited evangelism opportunities.

The reason? Man's physical needs offer opportunities to show the love of God and his care for persons. And loving care, the willingness to be involved, and the act of kindness may open a heart to receive God's salvation. A young woman, getting ready to leave the Seller's Home and Adoption Center in New Orleans, had just seen her baby, born a few days earlier, for the last time. As the social worker, who had returned the baby to the nursery, came back into the room where the young mother was, she found the girl standing at the window, weeping quietly.

During the months this daughter of a minister had been at Sellers waiting the birth of her child, she had seen the love and concern of the Christian workers in the Home. She had felt their care and protection. She received their counsel and guidance. She had heard and experienced in all of this the love and forgiveness of Christ in action. Now, in the final moments of her long wait, she could say to the social worker who had been her friend and counselor, "Today, for the first time in my life, I *know* God."

One technique most appreciated by Southern Baptists, promoted by Christian Social Ministries, is weekday ministries. These are dynamic forms and directions for presenting Christ's message compellingly to persons to whom that message is alien. They are used effectively not only by Baptist centers, many of which are supported in part by the Home Mission Board, but also by local churches.

In one church situation the leaders were convinced that their buildings should be used for more than the few hours they were occupied for structured worship and other church activities. The congregation enthusiastically supported a child care center and kindergarten program. Both, manned by efficient staffs, received the approval from the proper licensing services.

Working mothers found the day care center adequate in its provision for their children from early morning to late afternoon. A Christian atmosphere added to the distinctiveness of the service. Teachers talked and sang to the preschool children about Christ. The kindergarten classes provided a specialized teaching method not available elsewhere in the community.

Not a great many families became members of the congregation because of this effort, although some did. But an evangelistic witness was provided in other, less visible and less immediate ways. One family, professing to be atheists, enrolled a child in the specialized kindergarten. Contacts with this family offered the teachers opportunities to share the vitality of their Christian faith. Interested laymen gave tuition scholarships for many children who could not otherwise have been touched by Christian influence. Several people, seeing the church providing a needed service, were attracted to Christ by this demonstration of concern. Christians, who for years had been inactive in their commitments, renewed their vows to Christ through church membership. Several told the pastor that they were making these decisions because they had found a church that served.

Through weekday ministries some people are introduced for the first time to the meaning of Christian fellowship. One woman, whose family had been touched by such a ministry, said, "I had a hard life. My husband drank, and we never knew what it meant to have such friends as we have found in this place." The family had been sleeping on newspapers on the floor. Someone secured a job for the father and found food, clothing and furniture for the family. The mother became a member of a sewing class and the children were enrolled in kindergarten. The family gradually became a part of the church. There they met and had fellowship with their neighbors who were involved in church activity.

Faced with new and overwhelming needs, Christian Social Ministries has sought to minister creatively, experimentally, and, in some cases, even daringly to bring together man's need and God's love and power. Ministry in crisis situations, which includes witnessing to Christ's saving power, has been one channel of expressing this concern for man's total needs. In some centers someone is on duty twenty-four hours a day to offer help to people on the brink of suicide, to others broken with grief, to some on their latest "trip" on drugs or alcohol, to others embroiled in domestic difficulty.

In one crisis ministry a pastor walks the streets at all hours, watching for persons in need of Christian ministry. In other situations clinics have opened with doctors, dentists, lawyers and bankers who offer their services at stated hours to those who could not otherwise afford them. Many laymen have found their "handle" in this kind of ministry and have discovered a new way to give a Christian witness.

In one situation a pastor has been called to minister to

men and women from ten o'clock at night until six the next morning. He walks a prescribed beat, in and out of bars, to all-night eating places, to the police station, to gas stations, and to other places. He talks with countless persons, many of whom represent a crisis situation. To one and all he expresses in action as well as in words the love and concern of Jesus Christ.

In North Carolina a ministry began with the drug subculture. "Rap" sessions were opened, sponsored by all the churches of the city. Without preaching to them, ministers and other concerned Christians began to listen to the drug-addicts who came. The young people, many of whom had moved from marijuana to hard-core drugs, talked. They told of their emptiness, their sense of futility. The skills of professional help were made available to them. Christian witness was given, and many were pointed to and accepted faith in Christ.

In a more direct evangelistic outreach a youth revival, sponsored by a Texas church, was conducted under a tent during the summer. Many drug users, attracted to the evangelistic services, made professions of faith and gradually broke away from their experiments with drugs. But the most dramatic "happening" occurred in the life of a Christian layman. He attended the Saturday evening service, intent on criticizing the "long hairs" and the evangelistic effort in general. Instead he saw God's leadership in that evening's worship.

The layman caught a glimpse of what could be done with young people on drugs. He saw the power of the gospel to offer love and the promise of God's forgiveness to any person in need. He was impressed by the offer of professional help to those who needed medical and psychiatric attention.

The layman's life became a "vocation of concern." He opened his heart and his home to scores of young people trying to "kick the habit." He learned their language and became a crisis minister to dozens of them. He helped to organize a nonprofit organization which joined existing agencies in the city in the fight against drugs. Soon other concerned laymen in the city joined him in their investment of time, money and interest. At the last report, this work continued with great benefit. Because a Christian layman saw the challenge of ministry to persons and ran the risk of social involvement, many young people came to Christ.

Individuals and churches minister meaningfully to prisoners. For years laymen and pastors have conducted worship services in jails and other detention centers. But some states now allow model prisoners short paroles. They can be released to a family for a weekend. Many Christians have invited one or more prisoners into their homes and have brought them to Sunday worship and Bible study. A greater ministry, however, has often begun in the family setting itself.

A prisoner on "mini-parole" was welcomed into one Christian home. He accompanied the family to worship and was accepted in the church fellowship as a person of worth. The father found a way to prove that the acceptance was genuine in the simple crisis of his son's untied shoe laces. When the boy asked his father to tie his shoes, the father turned to the prisoner and said to his son, "Run to Bill. He'll tie them for you." When the child jumped down from Bill's lap the tears on the face of the man showed how much the confidence had meant.

It is no surprise that, after seeing Christian love in action, Bill became interested in the Christian faith. He saw something different in the lives of his new friends. Before many weeks had passed, Bill became a Christian and was baptized into the membership of the church that had come to mean much to him.

Released offenders have a great need for counseling, jobs, housing, help during crisis periods, emergency funds, tutoring, literacy classes and many other aids back to a useful life. A Christian businessman in the small city where the main unit of a state's correctional institutions is located, took a deep personal interest in every former prisoner he knew. Because he served as a probation officer, he had an excellent opportunity to know many of the men and women personally. For many years prior to his death, he sought jobs for these. In every way possible he encouraged and helped these people in their adjustment to the demands of society. He would never have thought of himself as much of a Christian witness. But he was, for many who needed his friendship found something genuine in him which can only be explained by the presence of Christ in a human life.

Another direction used to reach men with a witness of God's love is through literacy missions. Under the leadership of Mildred Blankenship, assistant secretary in the Department of Christian Social Ministries, this ministry has assumed major significance as a means of reaching persons for Christ. Typical of experiences resulting from this ministry is the story of a forty-eight-year-old man who was a true nonreader. Contacted by a literacy teacher, a member of a nearby church, the man began to learn the basics of reading and writing.

Shortly before he completed the first *Skill Book* he discovered that he had a malignancy on his back that would require surgery. He was anxious to complete this first book and receive his diploma for the step in his learning-to-read program, so he finished the course by attending class five times a week instead of only one time. A skin graft and 125 stitches later, the man again took up his eager effort to learn to read.

In the meantime, the church became involved with the entire family, providing assistance of various kinds. Among items given them was a copy of *Good News for Modern Man,* provided by the church missions committee. As the man progressed with his reading skill, he began to read the New Testament.

Within a month a blood clot on the lungs made a second

hospital experience necessary. But even during his convalescence his literacy study continued. During this time the church continued to minister to him and his family in many ways, ever showing their love and concern as well as Christ's love and concern for them.

Three months later all members of the family were regularly attending the nearby church. Later when the teacher took a Christmas arrangement to her student, again in the hospital, she commented that she did not know exactly what to get a man in the hospital. In answer, he reached over to pick up his copy of *Good News for Modern Man* and said, "You have already given me the best gift anyone could give." His wife added that he had told her he would not exchange what he had learned for a million dollars.

Not only does literacy offer an outreach ministry to functional nonreaders but it provides a Christian ministry and witness opportunity to Internationals in our country. Many of these people are temporary "guests" in the United States. Others have been induced by business, industry, and other attractions to settle here and become citizens. Many of these people do not know English. One woman, who had taken the literacy training under Miss Blankenship's leadership, invited a number of Japanese women who had just moved into a small city into her home. There she taught them the English language and some of the customs of America. The women responded with delight. They and their husbands were also invited to the social occasions at her church, where international suppers gave an opportunity to share native dishes and to enjoy a new circle of friends. The Christian woman listened for every opportunity to give her witness for Christ. And the church community always sought an opportunity to minister to all such people in the community. The evangelistic potential in such concern is evident.

Christian Social Ministries seeks to minister wherever men and women live out the concerns of their daily lives.

Each situation suggests its own unique program, and the opportunities are limitless. Some of these, in addition to the ones already mentioned, are among the aging, a group of increasing concern. Some opportunities are found among other groups: youth, unemployed, migrants, persons with mental and emotional needs, and others. All represent ways in which social concern can bear witness to God's love.

On the other hand, social action and evangelism are also closely intertwined. For years Southern Baptists have led in social action in the fight against such social blights as alcohol and gambling. Our denomination and many churches have also sought, through political and social activity, to eliminate other causes of human suffering and sorrow, but the need for greater involvement in this area of concern is great.

Christian laymen, for example, need positively to support national, state and city legislation which will help to assure greater opportunities for full life for all men. In one town, laymen from one church appeared at a meeting of the city council to voice their reasonable opposition to a particular proposal that was morally wrong because it was a threat to man's freedom. Some of the same laymen were present later to give their support to other proposals. Their presence and their argument for and against government action made a great difference for good. They spoke as concerned Christian businessmen, professionals and laborers. Their interest in the community was a witness for Christ. There is a great need for more Christians to live out their witness in the political arena.

A Southern Baptist church in Indiana provides an innovative social action through its bus ministry. Not only are their buses used to bring people to the services of the church. They are also used to carry voters to the polls!

There is an evangelistic potential in the interest of churches in better housing, more jobs and care for the poor. In affluent America, there are still more than twenty million people officially classified as living below the "poverty line." That figure reflects an increase of more than a million between 1971 and 1972.

Beverly Hammack, assistant secretary of the Christian Social Ministries Department of the Home Mission Board, talked about Christian responsibility in her address before the WMU Convention in Philadelphia in 1972. She spoke of a woman who sat in her mission action workshop only a month earlier. The woman, still in her thirties, had had eleven pregnancies and four miscarriages. Her children, one of whom sat on her lap, had never slept between sheets. She had stood for long hours in lines to get food stamps to buy meat, tainted enough to be colored like a rainbow. Her husband now suffered from a major heart problem. She could find no work. Her humiliation, tears and loss of self-esteem were the rewards of poverty.

Miss Hammack said that Christians must be concerned about confronting such people with the gospel. But she insisted that "we must also be involved in changing the society which grinds these persons into the dirt of crime and depravity. We must change social structure and come to grips with the cause of the social disease behind the problems. We must be concerned about unemployment, substandard housing, racial discrimination and other sources of suffering."

This is not the total Christian concern, however. A key to breaking the effects of poverty on an individual, the speaker continued, is to help him to know his Creator and to discover his own self-worth and personal value. The woman in Miss Hammack's workshop confirmed this when she said, "I have so much to live for. I have a hope and a drive given to me because I am a Christian."

Evangelism and social ministries indeed belong together. They are part of the one Christian mission. They serve one another in the Christian goal to make men disciples of Christ.

Chapter 4

a multilingual voice

Today one of the largest, single, "foreign" missions fields, encompassing a broad spectrum of the peoples of the world, lies within the borders of the United States. The 1970 government census revealed that there are some seventy-five million citizens, composing about 40 percent of the nation's population, who belong to some ethnic group.

Chicago alone has more than a million Polish people. New York, with more Puerto Ricans than are in San Juan, also boasts of more Jewish residents than the state of Israel has. Ocean Side, California, has the largest Samoan community outside the Samoan Islands. Miami ranks second to Havana in Cuban population. Twelve million Hispanic people, more than the population of some South American countries, live in the United States. As the doors of trade and travel open to China and Russia, doubtless more of the citizens of these nations will become a part of the American culture. This is indeed one world, and most of it is heavily represented in our country.

Primary Home Mission Board responsibility for outreach to ethnic groups whose language backgrounds are other than English falls to the Language Missions Department. Using every skill and understanding available from Interfaith Witness, Christian Social Ministries and Evangelism, the department assists Southern Baptists in seeking to enlist these representatives of other language backgrounds for Jesus Christ. One method adopted as a means of communicating the gospel message to the multiple ethnic groups concentrated in urban and metropolitan centers has been Evangelism's crusades, but with a multilingual character. Begun in 1971, a dozen such meetings had been held by 1972 in the United States and others were being planned for Panama and other places. Often a central crusade, multilingual in nature, is followed by revivals in ethnic churches. At other times, the order is reversed.

A thrilling story of such crusades comes out of New Britain, Connecticut. In this crusade people heard the gospel in eight different languages. Each night people worshipped in English, in the sign language, and in the Slavic languages. Simultaneously, services were conducted in Spanish.

E. L. Golonka, assistant secretary in the Language Missions Department, was not irreverent one evening when he whispered throughout the sermon to Rodney Webb, missionary to the deaf in the Northeast. A Polish sermon was in progress. A Russian woman, who is deaf, was present at the service, being conducted in the beautiful old home where the Slavic Evangelic Baptist Church met. Golonka translated the sermon into English. Webb "signed" the sermon for the Russian woman. Her face reflected the joy of "hearing" the gospel in her own unique language.

The music was furnished by the youth choir of the Green Acres Baptist Church of Tyler, Texas. Sixty-two young people did more than sing in the worship services. They conducted Vacation Bible Schools and visited in homes in the city each day. They won the support of the Salvation Army for the crusade because the choir assisted them in an unexpected overflow of children attending the Army's Vacation Bible School. They publicized the crusade and gave their own witness by appearing on a local color telecast. They sang at a civic luncheon, in a Slavic Pentecostal family encampment and in an open-air concert in the city park.

The entire city was caught up in the impact of this multilingual crusade. Rodney Webb visited the deaf. Vincenzi Coacci, missionary to the Italians in New England, witnessed among his people daily. This was New Testament evangelism in a unique community.

The evangelistic response was outstanding. A young Puerto Rican street leader who came to the Spanish services became a Christian. He told a choir member, "Thank you for coming to tell me about Jesus. If you had not come, I may never have heard."

Perhaps the most thrilling part of the crusade for the east Texas youth came after they had returned home. An alcoholic who had accepted Christ during the week hitchhiked all the way to Tyler. He arrived during the church service in which the choir shared the joy of their mission for Christ!

Multilingual evangelism has assumed additional importance through the training of laymen for witnessing. Soon after lay evangelism schools were begun and lay witness training methods were tested, it became evident that a large potential for lay evangelism existed in the ethnic groups of the nation. Calls for such lay training came from California, Texas, Arizona, Louisiana, Florida, and other states. Clearly the WIN materials which had been published in English needed to be translated into other languages. Daniel Sanchez, assistant secretary in the Language Missions Department, gave leadership to this work. Today these materials are available in Spanish and Chinese.

In the average multilingual training mission, English is

used either as the primary or secondary language. But the advantage of witnessing in their language to the unsaved among ethnic groups is apparent. In Chicago, Italian, Portugese and Polish pastors were involved in the telephone surveys designed to locate the unsaved. Every person called by one of these pastors was especially happy to converse in his native tongue. Many non-Christians were located who were responsive to the gospel.

The first person a Polish pastor called requested a visit to discuss his spiritual needs. Because the pastor could speak the man's native tongue, many misunderstandings were easily clarified. One woman asked, "What does it take to visit a Baptist church?" Evidently she felt that special qualifications were to be met before one could enter a Baptist church building! The pastor was able to explain clearly, because he used their common language, that no such restrictions exist. More important, he also had an opportunity to tell the woman of the openness of the gospel!

Many ethnic witnessing training schools for laymen are conducted. The methods which have stimulated laymen in other schools continue to prove effective. In Phoenix, in one of the small group sessions which are part of the lay evangelism school procedure, a Spanish-speaking woman found a unique way to describe her growing Christian maturity. Using pipe cleaners, devices designed to permit people to express themselves more creatively, she fashioned a rose bud. The flower, she said, represented the beauty of her life since she had received Christ. Then she portrayed the petals of the rose opening. This, she said, was a confession of her need to open her life more fully to Christ each day.

A Cuban in an Atlanta school used her pipe cleaners to form a coconut palm tree and placed a coconut at the top. She expressed a desire to climb the tree, to be near the delicious fruit and to have a more accurate view of all around her. In this way she spoke both of a desire to be closer to her Lord and to learn what this more intimate knowledge of him could mean for her total outlook on life.

Members of ethnic groups seem unusually responsive to the gospel at this time. When the leader of a lay evangelism school in Arizona visited in a Chinese home he received a typically warm welcome. The mother said, "I can't believe it! Only yesterday I felt an unusual burden about my relation to God. Last night I seemed to have an unexplained assurance that someone would come to tell me about Christ. How glad I am that God has sent you!"

Ethnic churches are growing as a result of multilingual evangelism. A lay evangelism school was scheduled for a church which was presently without a pastor. Little preparation for the school was possible. But twenty-five, in a congregation that was averaging only fifteen in Sunday School, attended the school. Two months later, the newly-called pastor reported that the twenty-five had already led twenty other persons to Christ. The Sunday School attendance had skyrocketed to one hundred and thirty-five. Optimism now prevailed throughout the congregation.

Spiritual vitality is deepening in ethnic churches because of the fresh emphasis on lay training and evangelism. Many congregations, frequently struggling in the past, have caught the spirit of outreach and new courage surges through them. The multilingual ministry proves the universality of man's spiritual need. It affirms a new openness to the gospel. And it demonstrates that the strategy for lay evangelism training and proclamation is effective with all groups.

Reaching today's man and communicating with him in the area of one's faith requires innovative approaches, especially when communication cuts across religious lines. At this point Interfaith Witness continues to make a creative contribution to evangelism, underscoring the concepts which predominate that department's philosophy of dialogue with other religions. M. Thomas Starkes, secretary of the department, identifies these as communication, demonstration and cultivation.

A willingness to hear others speak and the confidence that

all truth is incarnate in Christ helps the effective witness. People whose lives demonstrate the uniqueness of the Christian way of life make great impact on those who adhere to other religions. The Mormon who found his Baptist girl friend's life to be attractively different was convinced that there is something in Christianity, after all. She was open to hear about his own beliefs, and she lived out God's love in her everyday conduct. This is the value of demonstration in witness to all persons, but especially to those who are sharply at odds with the Baptist expression of the Christian faith.

A young Buddhist, "adopted" by a Baptist family in Atlanta, was accepted in the home. The true friendship and love which were extended to him were used of God to cultivate his interest in Christianity and to lead him to Christ.

Interfaith witness is a matter of finding common ground for conversation. It is friendship with a Jewish family for ten years before any one in the family received Christ. It is a pastor washing the car of a Jehovah's witness and later offering his services as parole officer for the same man's seventeen-year-old son. It is patient building of confidence. It is a witness to the uniqueness of Jesus Christ and his resurrection, while listening to and learning from the convictions of others.

Communication of faith reaches across more than just religious lines. Southern Baptists have long assisted black Baptists, mainly through the Home Mission Board's Department of Work with National Baptists. Now the focus on cooperation with black Baptists has been strengthened, as indicated by the change in the department's name January, 1973, to the Department of Cooperative Ministries with National Baptists. This department assists Southern Baptists in finding avenues of communication and ways of working together with National Baptists to strengthen the churches of both people. One of the areas in which study is being made is evangelism.

Emmanuel McCall, associate secretary of the department,

recognizes the fact that National Baptists usually do not employ some of the evangelistic methods used by Southern Baptists. Part of the reason for this is that they may not have developed these methods as yet. Southern Baptists can well enter into an equipping ministry with National Baptists, sharing methods and techniques with those trying to devise ways of making evangelism meaningful in the light of the accelerated emphasis on social concerns.

While National Baptists have been involved to some extent in evangelistic crusades and, more lately, in lay evangelism schools, they have been included for the most part only after plans have been finalized. There is a need, both from the standpoint of the all-inclusive nature of the gospel message and the equipping nature of our ministry, to include National Baptists from the beginning.

McCall challenges both blacks and whites to enter cooperatively into what he calls a Christo-centric evangelism. He points out that much of what has passed for evangelism in the past has not necessarily been Christ centered, but many times has been based upon regional or cultural similarities; educational, professional, or social status; and race. As an example, he shares a poignant experience from his own past. He remembers how he stammered and stuttered on one occasion while doing some evangelistic visitation as a pastor when he discovered a house occupied by whites. "My reaction," he says, "like that of other blacks, was related to the fear of being rejected. It never occurred to me that they might want to come to our church. While it, like most black churches, practiced open membership, I failed to give these families an adequate opportunity to make their own response."

McCall goes on to say that white Baptists need to help National Baptists become unafraid to witness to non-blacks; on the other hand, Southern Baptists need the help of National Baptists if they are to understand and witness to blacks. "What we all need," he says, "is some serious Christ-centered leadership in evangelism that is designed to people this world with 'kingdom men' who bear the image of Christ as illustrated in the Sermon on the Mount."

Efforts are being made toward developing this kind of Christ-centered cooperation. In Mississippi fifty black and white Baptist pastors and laymen met together in a meeting called a "human relations conference." Dick Brogan, Mississippi's director of work with National Baptists, chose the name because, he said, "man is basically a human being, and we need to relate to each other in Christ. I think of race as a biological matter and not as a spiritual term." Although the meeting was not altogether calm, Brogan sensed a new dimension and a new openness. Through efforts similar to this in spirit, we will learn to work together to claim this land for Jesus Christ.

Communicating one's faith to modern man must deal with changing life styles for everyone. This means that leisure-time must be considered as a major factor. As the working week has decreased, the leisure business has grown into a multi-billion dollar enterprise. The leisure culture threatens attendance and other regular patterns of worship and involvement, in many churches. Rather than reacting negatively to the new challenge, the Home Mission Board, through its Department of Special Missions Ministries, has developed a positive approach to it. This has provided Southern Baptists with outstanding evangelistic opportunities.

The initial step, in the late 60's, was to appoint summer missionaries to serve in resort areas. Using their ingenuity to meet needs in unusual situations, many of the young people found ingenious ways in which to witness. Their successes led to the appointment of home missionaries to a number of resort areas. Working on a year-round basis, these have been able to establish continuing programs of ministries that include recreation, Bible study, and worship experiences for all ages in vacation-type settings. From these ministries, many persons have found the Lord or have been won to a rededication of their lives to him.

Building on the success of this resort ministry, the Special Mission Ministries Department assigned responsibility for leisure and resort missions to Joel T. Land, assistant secretary in the department. Out of the background of his own experience as former pastor in the resort area of Mystic Island, New Jersey, Land has encouraged local churches in resort areas to establish ministries designed to attract vacationers and other persons who frequent these settings.

In the busy California resort area of Squaw Valley, for example, a former summer missionary serves a church that never closes its doors. Some nights the "street people" sleep in the building. On Sundays the two morning congregations worship in clothing which varies from cutoffs to business suits. During the week the church offers a quiet spot for meditation and prayer. But it also affords varied recreational activities, including Ping Pong and billiards for the young people who frequent its doors. On Saturday nights the building becomes a coffeehouse, where people with all sorts of backgrounds and problems feel free to "rap" and to be introduced to the Christian way of life.

Across the continent, in another type of situation, a Florida minister helped to form a "recreation ranch," where horseback riding, motorbikes and camping are made available to many on weekends. He conducts a worship service at the riding stable on Sunday mornings. One regular worshipper is a waitress who works every Saturday until midnight and feels that she can attend this open-air service more conveniently. Another is a chain restaurant manager who chose this type of worship deliberately. The campers who attend include a former motorcycle gang leader. A great many of the bike riders and horsemen are drawn to the worship because both the minister and the businessman-partner are well-known participants in the sports they also enjoy.

Some churches are too far away to be actually part of a resort area, but they are close enough to be interested and concerned. Many of these are establishing satellite churches at nearby lakes or other leisure spots. Some years ago—and perhaps some feel so now—many would have been negative about such approaches on the grounds that they represent a compromise of the sacredness of the Lord's Day. Without destroying the evident necessity for a day set apart for worship of God, churches can well be in the process of the first stumbling steps toward ministry and evangelism in a new world of leisure. Properly understood, this is only another means of outreach for contemporary Christians in their witness to the world.

Camping is an important phase of the leisure culture. Each year thousands of motorcycles, cars, campers and trailers streak along our highways to crowd to capacity campgrounds and resort areas all over the nation. In them, Joel Land sees unlimited witnessing opportunities. Because of this, Land has led Southern Baptists in an innovative outreach ministry called "Campers on Mission." Under this plan, individuals, families, and even groups may register with the Home Mission Board, committing themselves to be missionaries while camping and to use every opportunity they have to witness to their faith in Christ wherever they go. By 1973 more than eight thousand families, including youths and adults, had made such a commitment.

Opportunities to witness may come at the most unexpected moment. A Baptist, visiting the Seminole Indian Reservation in Florida, was looking at a picture of one of the Indian chiefs, in one of the gift shops. Also looking at the picture was a young Indian from Iowa.

"What does that mean?" the young man asked the Baptist, indicating the date A.D. 1871 beneath the picture.

When the Baptist man explained that A.D., date-wise, meant after the birth of Christ and that B.C. meant before Christ, the Indian asked who Christ was. He had heard of

God but had never heard of Christ. Later, in his trailer, the Baptist told the young man about Jesus and answered his questions. "He wanted to know more about Him," the man said. "I gave him my own New Testament with appropriate passages circled in red and instructions on how to find a right relationship with God." He also suggested that the Indian, who was visiting friends on the reservation, talk with Chief Osceola, a Seminole Baptist pastor on the reservation.

Sometimes meeting a need opens the door to a witnessing opportunity. Three college students, camping in a tent in a state park, found that they had forgotten to get bread. When they asked their neighbor-campers for some, they noticed the Campers on Mission sticker on the bumper of their car. Curious, the boys asked its meaning. The explanation led not only to the needed bread but also to an invitation to share the evening meal with the Baptist family. Over supper, they told the young men what Jesus meant in their lives both as a family and as individuals. The students, experiencing the mental and spiritual conflicts which many college students face, began to ask questions and to express some of their own needs. Before the young men returned to their tent, hours later, they each had found faith in Christ also.

Campers on mission often work directly with appointed Home Mission Board missionaries. One family with teenaged sons helped Coy Finley in Eagle Nest, New Mexico, with Vacation Bible Schools, campground services, a coffeehouse for youth, music and recreation. Although this is a remote resort area, campers from all over the nation fill the small mission church each Sunday during the summer months.

Not only do individuals and families become involved in this kind of outreach, but groups and even churches may organize as camping caravans. Paying all of their expenses, they travel in caravan fashion to assist a missionary with a project he has designed for them to do. They camp in a nearby campground, in church parking lots, or in some other camping spot during the one or two weeks they are there. Witnessing opportunities are innumerable as they assist with and even conduct mission Vacation Bible Schools, surveys, revival visitation, youth camps, public campground ministries, construction of new buildings, inner-city Baptist center work, and many other types of activities.

One church in the greater Louisville, Kentucky, area has many members who are campers. Twice a year, during the Fourth of July and Labor Day weekends, a large part of the membership leave the city on Friday afternoon. They go to one of the many beautiful camp facilities nearby and remain there until the following Monday afternoon. Regular worship services are conducted at the "home base," but usually twenty families at least are together at the campsite.

On Sunday mornings the church becomes campers on mission. They worship together and invite others in the camping area to join them. On a recent Labor Day weekend the church youth drama group presented an effective modern version of "Noah," and an unusually large number of campers joined in the worship. The opportunities for Christian witness go beyond the Sunday worship, as the swimming, fishing and relaxation fellowships offer all kinds of chances for the church to reach out in concern for those who do not know Christ.

The leisure culture offers a new challenge in other directions than just the resort areas, however. For some years deterioration due to the population rush to metropolitan centers has caused much concern to be focussed on our rural areas. For Southern Baptists, this has had a special impact, for congregations in the open country and small towns have been the predominant factors in the magnificent saga of our ministry. Now, however, as people leave the cities for leisure-weekend living or for permanent residence, the rural church stands before a new day of potential growth. The invasion of urban culture presents problems, but it also affords new opportunities for evangelism.

The Home Mission Board, through the Division of Associational Services, suggests that the methods of contemporary evangelism can be adapted to all churches, regardless of size or location. Under the leadership of Larry Bryson, associate secretary responsible for rural emphasis, much in-depth study has been undertaken in the future of rural and small churches. The nationwide Small Church Conference, held in 1973, under Bryson's leadership was an outgrowth of this kind of concern and assistance.

Many rural churches, sensing the new opportunities before them, are beginning to take on new life. Some excell in all forms of Christian mission, particularly at the point of evangelism. One rural church in Florida led the state in baptisms in 1970. Lay witness training and special social ministries had a great deal to do with this fact.

Because Southern Baptists have turned to new, creative ways of expressing our faith, in the seventies, the question might be raised: Have the newer expressions of evangelism outdated all of the methods of outreach with which we have long been familiar? Not at all! In fact, lay witness and evangelism training, social concern and action, and all the other innovative techniques that have proved effective in contemporary evangelism will give new vitality to every means of outreach which is viable for our time.

Southern Baptists are adopting new means of evangelism to enrich the old and to create the new in witness. By so doing, we are biblical. We follow Paul whose desire was to be made all things to all, that he might surely win some.

Chapter 5

contemporary channels

The contemporary mind-set and modern culture demand that Southern Baptists renew all that is biblical about evangelism and turn to every possible means of creative witness. But, while new techniques and methods of outreach have been devised, older and more familiar ones are still used with great success. They are made even more effective by fresh adaptations.

For example, crusades find new strength because of the renewal of lay involvement in witness, concern for the total man, and other phases of contemporary outreach. In 1972 the Division of Evangelism participated not only in planning and financing but in the follow-up ministry of twenty-four metropolitan and area crusades. Representing only a portion of the total led by staff members of the division, these were conducted in both well-established Baptist areas as well as in the newer areas, from Alaska to Bridgeport,

Connecticut, to Panama. Although the only measure of success in evangelism is certainly not numbers, the 2,464 decisions reported in the Panama crusade alone do indicate that the effectiveness of the mass crusade is not yet past.

One of the "grass roots" ministries with which the Evangelism Division has been working is the bus ministry. Long used by churches and missions as a means of bringing children and other persons to various activities, the bus ministry has now been seen as an opportunity for witnessing and evangelistic outreach. William Powell, the division's consultant in bus evangelism, works closely with the Sunday School Board in the total bus ministry.

Laymen are heavily involved in this form of outreach. They ride the buses as drivers, bus captains, secretaries and teachers. They visit in the homes of their children each Saturday, to demonstrate interest in the child and to contact other members of the family who need the ministry of the church. The actual time spent on the bus while driving to and from the church becomes a period of planned evangelistic ministry. Led by the lay team, who may include youths and adults, the activities include singing, personal dialogue and witnessing.

If the ministry is conducted correctly, the evangelism potential is great. Not only are children introduced to the Bible and to the worship of God, but their families are also touched by Christian witnessing. The bus ministry has its excesses, to be sure. Not every church will find it effective or needed. Young children are sometimes exploited to make decisions for Christ which they do not understand. Buses have been used only for the purpose of rescuing a church's sagging attendance. But, conducted correctly and motivated by concern for individuals, this ministry can be one of the most effective means of contemporary outreach.

The use of buses has resulted in growing Sunday Schools and churches. It is an outreach method which has reached many young people and adults for Christ. A pastor in Illinois reported the growth of his Sunday School by almost a hundred after a lay evangelism school and one month of a bus ministry. More than fifty persons had been baptized as a direct result of these two new efforts to reach beyond the church in evangelism and ministry.

An illustration of the effectiveness of the bus ministry comes from a Florida pastor. One of the young children who had become a part of the church family because he rode a bus every Sunday was struck by a car and killed as he walked home from elementary school. The bus captain was the first person to get to the family after the accident. He went with them to the hospital. He was with them during the difficult hours of arranging for the funeral. He shared the grief of the stricken family in every possible way.

Before the tragedy the family had demonstrated little interest in Christ or in the church. But the concern of the church at a time of great need helped to change all of that. Soon after the child's funeral the family began to attend worship. It was not long until the parents and several other members of the family were won to Christ and made public confessions of faith.

A retired seminary professor, who for years gave leadership to evangelism through the Sunday School, believes that the bus ministry is much more than a fad. He writes, "It may be God's way of helping us revive a New Testament compassion for reaching people with the gospel message in a contemporary, urban setting through the modern Sunday School."

For years telecasting has been a popular means of projecting Sunday morning worship services beyond the walls of church buildings. It has also been used in other ways. Some churches sponsor newscasts or buy thirty second "spots" which convey the Christian message in a different way. Many television and radio stations feature "the religious side of the news" programs weekly, during which ministers of various denominations dialogue on the issues of the day.

A Dallas church sponsors the radio broadcasts of certain sports events. But there are those who believe that there is vast potential for evangelism through the use of the mass media.

One of these is Kenneth Chafin who, as former director of the Evangelism Division, brainstormed the idea of a series of television shows that presents the gospel message for today's man. "Spring Street, USA," fast-paced and enjoyable, is Southern Baptists' first attempt at a religious variety-show format. The series, aired for the first time February 22, 1973, on a major network in eleven major metropolitan areas, seeks to blend the best of variety-show entertainment with short, relevant evangelistic messages. The series is arranged in thirteen weekly "installments" and is being shown in an increasing number of cities throughout the nation.

Produced for the Home Mission Board by the Radio and Television Commission, the telecasts are of high professional quality, with music under the direction of the well-known Buryl Red, a Baptist layman. A musical group, formed especially for the telecasts called the Spring Street Singers, appear each week along with such guest celebrities as Pat Boone, Ken Medema, Astronaut James Irwin, Dale Evans Rogers and others. Each program includes a short, timely, evangelistic message. Throughout, the Home Mission Board has been responsible for the content of the show while the Radio and TV Commission has applied its skilled expertise and experience in the production and distribution of the programs.

The Commission had already demonstrated the effectiveness of varied large-scale use of the mass media. Now, with the success of "Spring Street, USA," the future potential for evangelism is as great as the potential of the mass media themselves.

During the 1960's Southern Baptists, along with other Baptist bodies, were involved in a major evangelistic event: the Crusades of the Americas. Not only did these crusades involve the majority of other Baptist groups, but they spanned both the North and South American continents. During the early seventies Southern Baptists were again involved in a nationwide evangelistic effort called Key '73. This time denominational lines were crossed, with 115 different religious bodies including Roman Catholics participating in a continent-wide, yearlong evangelism emphasis in the United States.

Key '73 stemmed from a meeting called in the late 1960's by Carl F. H. Henry and chaired by Billy Graham "to explore the possibility of Christian denominations doing something together to seek a spiritual revival." It was agreed that America needs Christ and "that no one group of evangelicals could evangelize America alone." The central purpose of Key '73 was "to confront the people of North America with the call to follow Christ in faith and obedience." There was no doctrinal statement and no attempt to define evangelism. Each participant group, using its own methods and approaches, engaged in some project in evangelism in 1973.

Southern Baptist efforts focussed in plans suggested by a committee of which John Havlik, associate director in the Evangelism Division, was a member. They included giving priority to lay evangelism schools, renewal evangelism, youth evangelism and student evangelism. In addition to these, overall Southern Baptist Convention efforts included stressing evangelism through three emphases: People to People, Extend Now and Witness Now. Primarily the Sunday School Board and the Home Mission Board gave leadership to these, but implementation was carried out on individual state and associational levels.

In the January, 1973, issue of *Home Missions,* Arthur B. Rutledge, executive secretary of the Home Mission Board, writing of the rising tide of evangelism concern within Christian ranks in North America, said: "There seems to be a fresh openness to the gospel and an increasing interest in the Bible by hosts of people in our nation. . . .

"This is an opportunity for every Baptist and every Christian to pray for revival, work for revival, and give his best witness to the love of God in Jesus Christ." The old error, "if God wants to save anybody, he will do it himself," is always either an excuse for silence or a total misunderstanding of God's purpose for his people. His message of saving love can be told only as his people are willing to give themselves to the task of bringing unreconciled men to him through Christ Jesus.

But we must rely upon God's power for authentic evangelistic commitments; we *can not* make another's decision for him, or force that decision. The evangelist—whether he be a lay person, a preacher, or a full-time evangelist—must not be guilty of doing, in evangelism, what Jesus himself refuses to do: violate a person's right to remain free to decide for himself. Such "getting ahead" of God has been the weakness of much of the evangelism effort in the past.

To be authentic, evangelism is absolutely dependent on God's power. Its story in the New Testament is one of the achievements of which man is incapable. Luke, more than any other writer of the early church, described the factors in evangelism. The most important ones for him were the two that men cannot provide. The first of these is the Holy Spirit. He is God's resource standing with man's resources to make witness effective. He is the presence of Christ to energize witness and Christian living.

The relation of the Holy Spirit to witness is unmistakably clear in the New Testament. Jesus told his disciples that they were to wait for the "coming of the Spirit" before they launched their work for him (Acts 1:4–8). Luke, the historian of Christian advance over all barriers, was careful to relate every new victory of the unhindered gospel to the presence and power of the Holy Spirit. Jesus made it clear that only the Spirit can convict men of their need for salvation (John 16:8–11). He underscored the fact that no man can become a Christian without the work of the Holy Spirit (John 6:44).

Paul eloquently outlines man's salvation as the work of God the Father, of Jesus Christ the Son, and of the Holy Spirit (Eph. 1:3–14). He also reminds us of the necessity of God's presence in the Christian mission (1 Cor. 3:6,7): A Christian witness may plant a thought in a man's mind. Another Christian can bring a person near to Christ by cultivation. But, in the end, it is God who brings the unsaved to Himself. Evangelism is powerless without the presence of God. Paul goes on to assure us that it is from the Holy Spirit that all spiritual gifts come (1 Cor. 12:4–6). And it is the use of these gifts in the power of God's Spirit that makes for effective witness.

What does the Spirit of God, as the first necessary factor for evangelism, mean for us today? It not only means that no contemporary witness can be fruitful unless it is dependent on God; it also means that contemporary Christians must recognize the freedom of God to bring a revival of evangelism as he will. James Stewart, the remarkable Scottish preacher, makes this point in his sermon "The Wind of the Spirit." Speaking of Jesus' use of the symbol of the wind in his conversation with Nicodemus, Stewart declares that the wind stands for the sovereign freedom of the Spirit. "Just as it is impossible to control the wind or to dictate to it its direction, so no man, no church, can domesticate the Spirit of God or delimit His sphere of operation."

The story of God's movements in history is the story of surprises. God moves among people and in events which appear most unlikely, even to the most religious. The history of evangelism is the account of God breaking out in the most unlikely places, after institutional religion has eroded its usefulness into formalism and complacency.

Our knowledge of the power of the Spirit, who is necessary for evangelism, should make us slow to judge any movement or "new thing" in which persons are attracted to Christ. Has genuine revival begun in the movement of youth to express their faith so easily and in such new ways? While it may be too early to tell, it is well to recall how many great awakenings have begun among the young. Is the evangelistic renewal for which we pray to be achieved through new forms of worship or even through new forms of the institutional church itself? Whatever the answer, modern Christians who are hesitant to accept the new must remember that God's Spirit cannot be contained in any self-prescribed limits. Just as the wind, of which Jesus spoke in his encounter with the ancient ruler of the Jews, is always moving, so the Holy Spirit is free to move where he will!

The necessity for God's Spirit as the primary factor in evangelism means that Christians must be sensitive to God in their witness to others. We must ask for and wait upon the Spirit to lead us in any evangelistic witness. Many people who witness are ineffective because they "rush in where angels fear to tread." The maturing Christian is alert to the doors opened by the Holy Spirit for the sharing of the gospel. He trusts the Spirit to bring the witness experience to the moment for the appropriate sharing of Christ as the answer to the individual's needs.

The second factor in New Testament evangelism which Luke emphasized was the Word of God. In such Scripture as Philippians 1:19 and 1 Thessalonians 1:5, it appears that it is through the Word of God that the Spirit of God acts. By the Word of God, Luke and other New Testament writers meant the Word of John 1:1–18, Jesus Christ. The power for evangelism rests in the Person we proclaim. The Evangelist of the Gospels, Jesus, has become the Evangel, the message, of Christian witness.

A careful study of the sermons of Acts reveals a common content. Peter's sermon at Pentecost is a model (Acts 2:14–39). In this sermon Peter spoke of Jesus as the fulfillment of the Old Testament's expectation of a Messiah (vv. 16–21). He spoke of Jesus' life and ministry (v. 22). He emphasized Jesus' death and resurrection (vv. 23–32). He preached that the presence of the Holy Spirit in the life of the church is evidence of Christ's resurrection (vv. 33–35). On the basis of this witness, and in response to the people's plea for instruction as to what they were to do, Peter called for repentance, faith and baptism (vv. 37–39).

In similar form, changing to fit circumstances, Peter, Stephen and Paul proclaimed the gospel. Their sermons were not the repetition of a carefully constructed series of statements. But they preached Christ, the Word of God. The unchanging message of New Testament evangelism is that "God was in Christ, reconciling the world unto himself" (2 Cor. 5:19).

The Christian evangelist does not witness to himself or to an institution. He witnesses to Christ, if there is to be power in his effort. It is the work of the Holy Spirit to use the Word to confront man with himself and to move him to receive salvation.

Many unsaved persons have the idea that the Christian's interest in them is purely institutional. Perhaps this idea comes from our common misconception of what it is to witness. We should center our witness on a personal knowledge of Christ. Then, when men have received him, we should not hesitate to speak of the institution as a community of believers in Christ and to urge the new Christian to identify with a church.

Elton Trueblood, a pioneer in Christian renewal and evangelism, insists in his book, *The Validity of the Christian Mission,* that the missionary does not have a long creed. He does not need one. "He has only one commitment and that is to Christ. Believing that Christ is trustworthy, he allows the argument to go from there. . . . One of the most notable of missionaries, George Fox (1624–1690), is reported to have said, 'I took men to Jesus Christ and left them there.' "

The Word is necessary for power in evangelism because he is the Good News. Paul insisted, in his communication with the Corinthian church, "I determined to know nothing among you, save Jesus Christ and him crucified."

The necessity of the Word for power in evangelism has other meanings. The early Christians witnessed to a resurrected Christ. The fact that the Word was alive made their message powerful. Witness to Christ, therefore, is a witness to a Person who is doing something in human life and history today.

The term "Word" meant more than something spoken to the biblical writers. In the Bible "Word" means deed as well as Person. Christ is God's redemptive Deed. Thus, the Word can be demonstrated as well as spoken. One theologian, Culbert G. Rutenber, interprets the ministry of Peter and John to a beggar (Acts 3) in this manner: "What is God trying to tell us in all this? The answer marks the . . . beginning—God grant—of a new understanding of witness. Witness cannot be carried by words alone. If it is the love of Christ to which we would witness, we must *become* the love of Christ in incarnation and effectual deed in order to speak meaningfully of it."

The power for the task of evangelism is the Holy Spirit. It is also Christ, the Word which the Spirit uses. And it is Christian concern, a gift of the Holy Spirit to all believers who will receive it. If our land is to be won for Christ, the responsibility for the task must belong to each Christian. Yet it is fruitless to think that one can *determine* that he will be concerned about people. The early disciples were not evangelists because God commanded them to be. They witnessed out of their love for Christ and concern for the lost. And no concern for the lost can occur until we Christians permit the Holy Spirit to love other Christians through us.

A church newsletter carried an honest and tender confession of one so trapped by the busy life he lived that he neglected a final opportunity for concern. He had felt a strong impression to visit his sister's husband while on a trip to the Tennessee mountains. The brother-in-law, a minister, faced a crisis in his personal life and needed concern. But, like most of us, the man was too busy to follow his impression to visit with his relative and dear friend. A few days later the news came that the brother-in-law had died of a sudden and massive coronary.

There was time enough now to think of him and the burdens he had carried as a busy pastor, weighted with his own crushing needs. The brokenhearted Christian wrote about his experience, "It is a lesson in stewardship for me; one which I hope you will learn from *my* failure. Opportunity often comes our way but once; we need commitment to care. Commitment means never to have to say you're sorry." Multiply that man's regret and you will understand the need for the Christian to love those who need to hear and to know the good news of God's outreach for man in Christ.

Michael Green summarizes what modern Christians must do to recover the zeal and power in the evangelism of the early church. There will be no power until the world sees the caring, the joy, the fellowship, the self-sacrifice, and the openness that existed in the New Testament church. No progress in evangelism will be made until the truth is grasped that evangelism is the responsibility of every Christian and is supported by lives which are better than the best that unbelief has to offer. The Christian message must once again be centered in Christ. Each of us must use every means at our disposal to share Christ with others.

The issues of evangelism—the lostness of man, the uniqueness of Christ, the power of faith, and God's purpose for individuals and for the world—must be taken seriously.

QUESTIONS

Chapter 1

1. How are laymen motivated in evangelism?
2. What is a lay evangelism school?
3. What evidences indicate the appeal of lay evangelism schools?
4. What is renewal evangelism?
5. What do you think is the most exciting thing about renewal evangelism?

Chapter 2

1. What effect have young people had on the evangelistic movement in the last decade?
2. List three characteristics of the college scene in the early seventies.
3. How has the Division of Evangelism attempted to meet the needs of college students?
4. What is the difference between high school students of the sixties and those of the seventies?
5. Briefly list three important phases in the beach evangelism ministry.

Chapter 3

1. What is the relationship between evangelism and Christian social ministries?
2. What was Jesus' attitude toward social ministry?
3. List four examples of Christian social ministries having evangelistic results.
4. Briefly tell the story of one layman involved evangelistically in social ministries.
5. Why do evangelism and social ministries belong together?

Chapter 4

1. List three ways Language Missions is involved in evangelism.
2. How can faith be communicated across racial lines?
3. Tell briefly how resort missions became an evangelistic opportunity in at least one situation.
4. What is the purpose of Campers on Mission?
5. Do new creative ways of expressing our faith outdate all older methods of outreach?

Chapter 5

1 Can a bus ministry be a channel for evangelism?
2. What two fresh approaches to evangelism were used in 1973?
3. What does evangelism need to be authentic?
4. What is the second factor in New Testament evangelism?
What are the issues of evangelism, and what should be our attitude toward them?